Abigail Booth

Eat Well, Feel Great

25 Healthy, Satisfying Recipes
to Help You Look Fabulous
and Feel Amazing

Vitality Health Coaching

Nothing Tastes as Good as Healthy Feels

Published by Old Mate Media
www.oldmatemedia.com

Printed in Great Britain

ISBN 978-1-925638-21-9 (Print)
ISBN 978-1-925638-20-2 (Kindle)

Contents

The Philosophy Behind Eat Well, Feel Great

Eat Well, Feel Great will show you that delicious and nutritious food doesn't have to be boring, bland or complicated. That to look and feel great you don't have to starve yourself or use willpower to get there. You can eat healthy satisfying meals made of real food and still lose weight and have loads more energy.

Of course it isn't easy to juggle the demands of a career, family, home and social life (if you're lucky!) and then put a freshly cooked meal on the table each night but with a bit of organisation each week you can embrace a healthy balanced diet and lifestyle as well as cooking foods that all the family will enjoy.

I hope these recipes will inspire you to get creative in the kitchen using real wholesome foods such as protein, 'good' fats, plenty of fresh fruit and vegetables and wholegrains.

I try to avoid refined sugar and white flour as well as fried and processed foods as much as possible.

This doesn't mean you can never eat them – as soon as you tell yourself you can't have something you'll want it even more! But the more you experiment with delicious, real food the more you 'crowd out' the unhealthy choices. By experimenting and expanding your repertoire, as well as the ingredients you stock in your kitchen, you leave little room for the rushed convenient choices which are easily made when you haven't the time, energy or willpower to think!

Of course when you do fancy a sweet treat you will find some healthier alternatives in here that are just as satisfying.

Throughout the book I'll also share with you a few of the tips and tricks I use with my clients that are simple, effective and sustainable but can have a huge impact on your health.

Remember, long term healthy living doesn't have to be difficult or complicated – you can eat well and feel great through delicious, real and filling foods – go on give it a try!

Want more fabulous recipes?

I'm so excited to share these 25 recipes with you in this book, and I'm even more excited to let you know that there are more recipes available on my website. Just visit http://vitalityhealthcoaching.co.uk/abbys-kitchen/ to find even more healthy goodness for you and your family. You can also find me on social at:

f vitalityhealthcoaching1

◙ vitality_health_coaching

𝓟 vitalityhealthcoaching

Breakfasts

Baked Banana, Berry and Peanut Butter Oats

Despite this having quite a number of ingredients it really is quick and simple to make. It only takes 10 minutes to prep and then you have 4 breakfasts all ready and waiting.

For those of you who don't have time to sit down to eat in the mornings this is ideal as it can just be popped into a tupperware and eaten at your desk or even in the car!

Prep time: 10 minutes.
Cooking time: 50 minutes.

Ingredients:

SERVES 4–5

Coconut oil for greasing

180g oats

1 1/2 tsp baking powder

1 tsp ground cinnamon

1 tsp vanilla extract

2 tbsp. peanut butter (any nut butter will work equally as well)

2 tsp. honey (I have started making this without any honey at all and it still tastes as good)

2 eggs, beaten

220ml almond milk

2 bananas – 1 mashed and the other sliced for the top

150g frozen berries plus extra for decoration

flaked almonds to garnish

Method

1. Preheat oven to 200 degrees / 180 fan/ gas mark 4.

2. Grease a large casserole dish with coconut oil.

3. Combine the oats with the cinnamon and the baking powder in a large mixing bowl.

4. Then add the rest of the ingredients – vanilla extract, peanut butter, honey, eggs, milk, mashed banana and frozen berries.

5. Combine thoroughly and transfer into the casserole dish.

6. Decorate the top with sliced banana and the additional berries plus a sprinkling of flaked almonds.

7. Bake in the oven for 50 minutes until the top is golden brown and a skewer comes out dry.

8. Remove from oven and leave to cool for 10 minutes before cutting.

Family Friendly Pancakes

These are the simplest yet healthiest pancakes you will ever come across; ideal as either a breakfast or a dessert. Made with only 3 ingredients and your favourite toppings, they have been a hit with both toddlers and adults whenever they have been served!

Ingredients:

MAKES 3 PANCAKES

2 eggs
1 banana (the riper the better)
1 dessert spoon coconut flour
1 tsp coconut oil
Toppings of choice – I used natural yoghurt & blueberries

Method
This is so easy!

1. Put the banana into a bowl and mash with the back of a fork.

2. Then add the eggs and flour and whisk together with the fork until the mixture is as smooth as possible and no big lumps of banana.

3. Heat a 1 tsp of coconut oil in a frying pan until hot then add the pancake batter in 3 spoonfuls into the pan.

4. Cook on a gentle heat for a couple of minutes on each side ensuring it is cooked through in the middle but not burnt.

5. Serve with toppings of your choice.

Egg and Chorizo Hash

Despite chorizo being quite a fatty meat, so not one I would recommend being eaten too often, this does make for a yummy breakfast on a Sunday and will keep you full for ages too.

Plus it does contain some veg!

Ingredients:

SERVES 2

1 large red onion, chopped

1/2 chorizo sausage (approx. 100g), chopped into 1/2 discs

1 clove garlic, chopped

400g tin chopped tomatoes

paprika & chilli powder to taste

4 eggs

Method

1. Put the chopped onion and chorizo into a frying pan on medium heat. No oil is required as the chorizo creates enough of its own.

2. Gently fry until the onion is starting to soften – about 5 minutes. Then add the garlic and fry for a further minute.

3. Next add the chopped tomatoes followed by enough paprika and chilli flakes depending on how hot you like it.

4. Reduce the heat and leave to cook through gently for about 10 minutes until sauce has started to thicken.

5. As best you can make 4 little wells in the mixture and add in the eggs. Cover with a lid and leave to cook until the whites have set – about 5 minutes.

6. Serve.

What is Health Coaching?

As a Health Coach I teach the philosophy of eating slowly, enjoying mealtimes and eating until you feel satisfied rather than eating until you are full and zapped of energy. I want people to realise that looking and feeling great isn't about a short term quick fix deprivation diet – it is a lifestyle. By making small changes and embracing healthy, varied and fresh food you can live a balanced, healthy life that requires little effort but provides a lifetime of benefits.

What's important is working out what foods are right for you. Some people require bigger portions, others may have intolerances – don't be afraid to play around with these recipes to suit you. I haven't calorie counted them because I believe that if you are eating real, wholesome food and in portion sizes that are right for you, you don't need to worry about calories – they work themselves out.

Soups

Courgette, Soya Bean and Parmesan Soup

In challenging my clients to try new foods I decided to try soya beans myself.

These just came in a frozen packet so it was really easy and if you want to make this even easier you can even buy frozen courgettes too!

Although the recipe has bacon in it for the topping, this can easily be removed for vegetarians.

Ingredients:

SERVES 4

1 onion

1 tsp coconut oil

1 clove garlic

4 rashers bacon

220g soya beans for soup and 100g for topping

220g new potatoes, peeled and chopped into chunks

220g frozen courgettes

1.2 litres vegetable or chicken stock (2 cubes)

50g parmesan

salt & pepper to taste

150g crème fraiche

Method

1. Preheat oven to 200 degrees / 180 degrees fan/ gas mark 4.

2. Meanwhile finely chop the onion and heat the coconut oil in a large casserole/ soup pan on the hob. Add the onions to the pan and gently fry for about 5 minutes until starting to soften.

3. Once the onions are soft then add the garlic and fry for a further minute.

4. Next chop the bacon into small pieces and lay out on a baking tray with 100g of soya beans. Put into the oven for 15 minutes then give them a good mix and put back in the oven for a further 15 minutes until both the bacon and beans are crispy.

5. Add the potatoes, courgettes and stock to the pan on the hob, cover, and bring to the boil. Reduce heat and simmer for 10 minutes.

6. Finally add the remaining soya beans to the soup and cook for a further 10 minutes.

7. Once cooked through blend the soup with a hand blender and add the parmesan and seasoning leaving a little for the top.

8. Mix in the crème fraiche on a very low heat and if it goes lumpy for any reason then just give it a quick blitz again with the blender.

9. Serve with the crispy bacon and beans mixture and a little parmesan on top.

Turkey Meatball Soup

This is a lovely light summery soup and nothing like the heavy winter based soups we tend to crave when it's cold. It's simply made of tasty meatballs with plenty of veg in a stock broth making it ideal for a warm evening.

Feel free to swop out any of the veggies with alternatives from your fridge that need eating up.

Ingredients:

SERVES 4

1 tbsp. coconut oil

1 pack of 12 turkey meatballs

1 onion, finely diced

3 cloves garlic, finely diced

2 carrots, peeled & diced

2 stalks celery, diced

1 stalk fresh thyme leaves or 1 tsp dried thyme

1.2 litres chicken stock

2 large handfuls (approx. 100g) spinach

Method

1. Heat the coconut oil in a large casserole pan on the hob and add the meatballs. Cook on high heat, moving constantly to avoid sticking, until browned all over. They do not need to be cooked through at this point. Once browned transfer to a side dish.

2. Keeping the remaining oil and any turkey bits, add the onion, garlic, carrots and celery to the pan. Cook through on medium heat for about 5 minutes until starting to soften but not brown.

3. Next add the thyme, chicken stock and the meatballs. Bring back to the boil then reduce heat and simmer on low heat for about 15 minutes until meatballs are cooked through and vegetables are soft.

4. Lastly add the spinach and stir through until wilted. Serve.

Quick and Easy Minestrone Soup

This soup is a great way to use up lots of odds and ends of various veg plus it gets lots of your 5 a day into your meal – even my two year old doesn't notice as they are so soft!

The addition of pasta ensures it is filling enough for a lunch or a dinner. I always make plenty and heat it up the next day.

Ingredients:

SERVES 4

1 large or 2 small brown onions
2 cloves garlic, finely chopped
1 large carrot
1 courgette
1 stick celery
1 red pepper
2 stalks fresh thyme, leaves removed to use

4 -6 mushrooms
1 tbsp. coconut oil
400g tin tomatoes
1 litre chicken or veg stock (2 cubes)
4 leaves cavolo nero, hard stalk removed & leaves chopped
100g pasta (I use brown rice or buckwheat versions but you can also use whole-wheat)
400g tin cannellini beans
crème fraiche to serve (optional)

Method

1. Wash or peel the onion, garlic, carrot, celery, courgette, red pepper and mushrooms and chop into small pieces.

2. Heat coconut oil in a large casserole pan and gently fry the onions for a few minutes before adding the garlic. Cook through for 2 minutes on low heat before adding the carrot, celery and courgette.

3. Add the red pepper and thyme then the mushrooms and keep cooking gently. You can be a bit rough about cooking times as they will all cook through and soften nearer the end when the liquid and pasta is added.

4. Next add the tinned tomatoes and stock, bring to the boil and then reduce the heat, cover, and leave to simmer on low for 15 minutes. It can be left longer at this point if need be but not once the pasta has been added as it goes soggy.

5. Lastly add the cavolo nero, pasta and beans and cook for 10 minutes until the pasta is cooked through but not any longer.

6. Serve with crème fraiche (optional).

Get moving!

Find a way to get moving each day.

It doesn't have to be formal exercise if that doesn't float your boat – just try and move more – dance to your favourite music, get a hula hoop or even just take a quick walk on your lunch break.

If you have kids, chase them around the house, or play a quick game of catch. Remember every little bit counts.

Step trackers are a great way to set yourself mini goals which you can aim to beat each week and can be a great way to get social with friends too.

Salads

Roasted New Potato and Pancetta Salad

New potatoes are in season during the summer months so this is a great way of making a salad more interesting and more filling than boring leaves!

Feel free to add your own salad ingredients to it according to what you like or have in the fridge.

Ingredients:

SERVES 2

Approx 12 new potatoes

1 red onion, cut into wedges

2 sprigs rosemary

olive oil (approx. 1.5 tbsp.)

1 pack chopped pancetta (65g)

glug of red wine vinegar or balsamic vinegar

60g pecan nuts (feel free to substitute with others in your cupboard but I think these go the best)

salad ingredients of your choice such as rocket, tomatoes, cucumber

Method

1. Preheat oven to 220 degrees / 200 degrees fan/ gas mark 7.

2. Wash the potatoes and cut the large ones in half, the smaller ones can remain whole. Cook in a pan of boiling water for 10 minutes making sure that they don't go too soft.

3. Drain the potatoes and transfer into a roasting tin. Add the onion and rosemary.

4. Toss the olive oil in with the potatoes ensuring they are evenly coated and season to taste.

5. Roast in the oven for 45 minutes, turning over half way, until crisp and golden.

6. About 10 minutes before the potatoes are ready, fry the pancetta on high heat (no oil needed) until crispy. Add the vinegar to the pan, reduce the heat and stir well to get all the bits up from the bottom of the pan.

7. Put all the salad ingredients into bowls then add the pecan nuts, potato and onion mixture and add the crispy pancetta to the top.

8. Use additional olive oil to dress.

Chicken and Quinoa Salad

This is a really quick and easy meal option that is great packaged up and taken for a lunch. It is also just as good with goats cheese instead of the chicken for a variation.

I've put quantities of veg below but to be honest you can just use what you've got in your fridge or whatever you fancy that day -it's a really versatile dish.

Ingredients:

SERVES 2–3

2 chicken breasts

1 packet of ready made quinoa (you can use the dried version but it just takes longer!)

1/2 red onion, finely chopped

1/2 red pepper, chopped

8 – 10 cherry tomatoes, halved

100g frozen peas

100g frozen sweetcorn

Method

1. Pop the chicken breasts under the grill for 20 minutes turning them once. You know they are cooked when there is no pink meat inside.

2. Meanwhile chop the onion, red pepper and tomatoes and put the sweetcorn and peas into a steamer to cook for about 3 minutes.

3. Lastly put the quinoa packet into the microwave as per the instructions (normally 1-2 minutes).

4. Finish by mixing the quinoa, chopped veg, sweetcorn and pea mixture and the chicken together in a bowl and serve. It's that easy!

Duck and Puy Lentil Salad

I'm always looking for ways to make salads a bit more interesting and this is one of them.

Duck breast with puy lentils is tasty and filling and definitely brightens up boring leaves!

Ingredients:

SERVES 2

2 skin on duck breasts
50g dry puy lentils
1 chicken stock cube
50g pecan or pistachio nuts
rocket or other leaves
10 cherry tomatoes, halved
1/2 red onion, thinly sliced
cucumber slices

Method

1. Preheat oven to 220 degrees / 200 degrees fan/ gas mark 7.

2. Pat the skin of the duck dry with kitchen towel and score the surface several times.

3. Next place the duck breasts skin side down into a cold frying pan and cook on medium heat for about 8 minutes until the skin is golden brown. Then turn over and seal the other side for 30 seconds. Pour away any excess fat.

4. Whilst the duck is cooking heat a pan of water to boiling on the stove and add the lentils, stock cube and enough water to cover the lentils about 3 times over. Reduce heat and allow to simmer for 25 minutes until soft but not squishy.

5. Once sealed move the duck breasts onto a baking tray skin side up and cook in the oven for 12-20 minutes depending on preference (18 minutes is medium well).

6. While everything is cooking prepare the salad ingredients – leaves, tomatoes, onion and cucumber then add the nuts to the top.

7. Once cooked, cut the duck into slices and place on top of the salad. Scatter the lentils over the top.

Rest is essential

Sleep is absolutely essential in helping our body restore and detoxify itself overnight.

Ensure you eat at least 2-3 hours before bed so that your body isn't trying to digest your last meal instead of resting.

Another good tip is to take some power down time before bed and to switch off any electronic devices and do something pleasurable and relaxing such as taking a hot bath with candles, reading a book, meditating or some gentle stretching.

A good night's sleep will have you leaping out of bed in the morning!

Main Meals

Poached eggs with Spicy Chorizo and Cannellini Beans

This recipe either makes a great weekend breakfast or a mid-week supper – you choose.

Depending on how hungry you are either use 1 or 2 eggs per person and use as much or as little paprika as you fancy to add some spice.

Ingredients:

SERVES 2

1/2 spicy chorizo ring, cut into chunks

1 red onion, cut into chunks

400g tin cannellini beans

paprika, to taste

10 cherry or pomodore tomatoes, halved

200g spinach

4 eggs

black pepper

Method

1. Put the chorizo chunks into a food processor and blitz until crumb like. Then tip into a frying pan, no oil, and gently fry.

2. After a couple of minutes the pan will start to look oily so add the onion and cook for about 5 minutes until starting to soften.

3. Next add the cannellini beans and as much paprika as you want to add some spice.

4. Meanwhile put a large pan of water onto boil for the eggs. People make poached eggs in many different ways and I have these fantastic cups that float in the saucepan and make me great eggs each time. But if you don't have anything like that you can just swirl the water in the pan and add the egg directly to the middle. Cook for about 3 minutes until the whites are set but the yolk is still runny.

5. While the eggs are cooking add the tomatoes to the bean mixture as well as the spinach. You might have to add the spinach in batches and wait until it wilts down before adding the next lot. Stir thoroughly.

6. Once cooked remove the eggs with a slotted spoon and drain on kitchen paper.

7. Serve the bean mixture onto plates and top with the eggs and a grinding of black pepper.

'As Healthy as I Can Get it' Toad in the Hole

As his favourite dish, my Brother challenged me to make a healthy version.

I can't change that it's sausages in batter but I've made a few adjustments that mean it's still as tasty but a little bit healthier!

I've added onions, tomatoes & thyme to get some vegetables in there, I have used the best quality sausages I could find and the batter is gluten and dairy free as I have used almond milk and gluten free flour.

Ingredients:

SERVES 4

8 good quality sausages
2 red onions, cut into wedges
1 tbsp. olive oil
20 cherry tomatoes
few sprigs fresh thyme

For the batter:
4 eggs
220ml unsweetened almond milk
175g gluten free flour
salt and pepper to taste

Method

1. Preheat oven to 200 degrees / 180 degrees fan/ gas mark 6.

2. Put sausages, onions and olive oil into a large roasting tin and put in the oven for 20 minutes turning over half way to ensure sausages are browned all over.

3. Meanwhile make the batter. Put the eggs, milk and flour into a large mixing bowl and briefly whisk until all evenly mixed.

4. After 20 minutes remove the sausages and as many onions as possible from the roasting tin and temporarily set aside. Pop the tin back in the oven to ensure the remaining oil is as hot as possible (if necessary add a little more).

5. Once heated back up, pour the batter directly into the tin and then place the sausages, onions and tomatoes on top letting them sink into the batter. Scatter the thyme on top.

6. Place the roasting tin back into the oven and cook for about 30 minutes when the batter should have risen and look golden brown on the top and a skewer comes out clean.

7. Serve with some green vegetables for extra goodness.

Crispy Chicken, Sweet Tomatoes & Cheesy Polenta

This is a wonderfully light and easy dish to whip up in an evening and even better to sit and eat al fresco.

The polenta is naturally gluten-free and low fat and is great at absorbing flavours so this makes a lovely alternative to pasta or rice.

Ingredients:

SERVES 3

500g pack ready-made polenta

25g parmesan, finely grated

3 skin-on chicken breasts

250g sweet cherry tomatoes

2 springs rosemary, leaves torn off

2 garlic cloves, thinly sliced

2 tbsp olive oil

Method

1. Preheat oven to 220 degrees / 200 degrees fan/ gas mark 7.

2. Using your fingers roughly break the polenta up into small chunks and scatter in the bottom of a roasting tin.

3. Tip in the parmesan and mix.

4. Sit the chicken breasts (skin side up), cherry tomatoes, rosemary and garlic on top of the polenta.

5. Drizzle with olive oil and season to taste.

6. Roast for about 30-35 minutes until the chicken is crisp and golden and the polenta is starting to turn crispy around the edges.

Butternut Squash, Red Pepper & Quinoa Chilli

This recipe was inspired by a meal I had recently at a Gastro Pub near to me.

It's a great veggie meal but lighter than traditional vegetarian chilli and really different.

I served it with crispy tortillas which add some crunch and are great for dipping!

Ingredients:

SERVES 6

1 brown onion
2 cloves garlic
1 fresh chilli
1 tsp coconut oil
1/2 large or 300g butternut squash
1 red pepper
50ml red wine (optional)
400g tin chopped tomatoes
1 tsp turmeric
1/2 tsp paprika
1/2 tsp cayenne pepper (only if you like it hot!)
300g uncooked quinoa
800ml veg stock (1.5 cubes)
400g tin red kidney beans in chilli sauce
6 wholewheat tortillas
olive oil for brushing

Method

1. Finely chop the onion, garlic and chilli. Then heat the coconut oil in a large casserole pan and gently fry the onions until they are starting to soften before adding the garlic and chilli. Cook for a further few minutes.

2. Meanwhile chop the squash and pepper into small chunks (approx. 1cm) and add to the pan. Cook through for a few minutes before adding the red wine (if using). Allow this to boil off for a few minutes.

3. Next add the tinned tomatoes and spices and mix thoroughly before adding the quinoa and 500ml of the veg stock (1 cube). Stir, cover and leave to simmer on very low heat for 20 minutes. Stir occasionally to ensure it doesn't stick.

4. Lastly add the kidney beans in their sauce and the last of the stock. It can either be served now or left on very low heat until ready to serve. If you leave it longer it may need more water adding as the quinoa absorbs lots of water!

5. To make the crispy tortillas simply pre-heat the oven to 200 degrees/180 fan/gas mark 6. Brush each tortilla on one side with olive oil and pop in the heated oven for about 3 minutes until starting to brown and go crispy.

Grilled Chicken with Bacon and Pine Nut Cabbage

This recipe was inspired by a dish that my friend Hilary makes but I've added some garlic for an extra taste hit.

It's really easy to make and a great source of protein with the cabbage providing over half your daily Vitamin C requirements!

Using the pine nuts will give you a source of healthy fats to keep you full in the absence of starchy carbs.

Ingredients:

SERVES 2

2 chicken breasts
6 slices streaky bacon
1/2 large savoy cabbage or whole small one
2 cloves garlic, chopped
2 large handfuls pine nuts

Method

1. Put the chicken breasts to cook under the grill.

2. Meanwhile chop the bacon into bite sized pieces and roughly shred the cabbage then wash it.

3. Put the bacon, without any oil, into a wok or frying pan and cook on a high heat until crispy (approx. 5 minutes).

4. Once cooked remove with a slotted spoon and put aside. Try and leave as much of the fat in the bottom of the pan as we will use this to cook the cabbage and give it extra flavour.

5. Next put the cabbage into the pan and stir fry it on high heat. If there is too much cabbage to fit into the pan initially then just wait until the first batch has started to wilt and then add more in. Keep doing this until it all fits – it will do eventually!

6. Once all the cabbage has started to wilt then add the garlic and pine nuts. Continue to cook for a few minutes on high heat.

7. Lastly add the bacon and stir through ensuring it is evenly mixed.

8. After about 20 minutes check the chicken is cooked through by ensuring there is no pink showing in the middle.

9. Serve the cabbage mixture topped by the hot chicken breast. A delicious nutritious meal on the table in 20 minutes!

Take Time to Meal Plan

I know you're busy…. most people are these days.

But…..we all make time for what's important to us.

Instead of scrolling down Facebook for the third time today or watching an extra episode of your favourite TV show why not spend 30 minutes a week planning your meals and placing an online shopping order?

Once you have a core menu of meals for you and your family the job becomes much easier.

I encourage my clients to have a 6 week rolling meal plan to make things even quicker and if you want to try something new a particular week then just swap out one of the regular recipes.

Plus I have just the thing to help you……

Grab your
Bonus Happy Healthy You
Starter Kit today!

Plus I'll send you regular motivation and support to help you along the way.

The Starter Kit includes:
• 3 Simple Top Tips to make a difference today!
• Printable Meal Planner
• Guide to Healthy Snacks on the Go
• Delicious and nutritious recipes.
Join by visiting the website below

vitalityhealthcoaching.co.uk/happy-healthy-you-starter-kit/

Pork Kung Po Stir Fry

A very quick and easy pork stir fry that tastes divine! This meal will give you several portions of veg plus a good protein hit. The fats in the pork, egg and olive oil will help keep you full as there are no extra carbs in this recipe.

If preparing for children, add a small portion of brown rice with it to ensure they are getting their energy requirements.

On the table from scratch in 30 minutes flat!

Ingredients:

SERVES 4–5

1 red onion
1 medium courgette
1 pepper
1 pak choi
4 -6 mushrooms
2 tsp olive oil
500g pork mince
2 tsp paprika
2 tsp turmeric
1 tsp curry powder
2 cloves garlic, finely chopped
½ bag beansprouts
1 tbsp tamari (or soy sauce)
2 tbsp oyster sauce
1 egg, beaten
Either spinach or lettuce leaves to serve

Method

1. Chop the onion, courgette, pepper, pak choi and mushrooms into small bite sized pieces.

2. Heat the olive oil in a wok or large frying pan and add the pork mince. Cook on medium heat until starting to brown. Drain off any excess water that accumulates before adding the paprika, turmeric, curry powder and garlic and mix in.

3. Once the pork has browned then add the onion, courgette and pepper and cook for a few minutes.

4. Next add the rest of the vegetables – pak choi, mushrooms and beansprouts and cook for a further few minutes.

5. Finally add the tamari, oyster sauce and egg and thoroughly mix to ensure everything is evenly coated.

6. Line the bottom of your bowls with either spinach leaves or lettuce leaves and serve the stir fry hot on top.

Healthy Pulled Chicken Burgers

I was recently asked if I could find a way of making BBQ sauce healthy.

So I came up with this sugar-free BBQ style marinade and made pulled chicken.

You would never believe it's just tomato puree and herbs with a tiny bit of honey to taste – give it a go, it's a great family dinner without any guilt!

Ingredients:

SERVES 4

4 chicken breasts (approx. 150g each)

500ml vegetable or chicken stock

4 spelt / rye/ grain buns

4 tbsp. tomato puree

1 ball low fat mozzarella

16 cherry tomatoes

large handful of spinach

1/2 red onion

For the marinade:

4 tbsp. tomato puree

3 tbsp. honey

1 tsp paprika

3 tsps. oregano

1.5 tsp onion powder

1.5 tsp garlic powder

4 tsp balsamic glaze

salt and pepper to taste

Method

1. Preheat grill.

2. Then bring a large pan of the stock to the boil and add the chicken breasts in. Ensure there is enough water to cover the chicken- if not add a little more. Cook for about 15 minutes until there is no pink inside the chicken. Drain and remove from the heat.

3. Meanwhile make up the marinade. Put all the ingredients together in a small bowl and mix thoroughly into a paste.

4. Take the chicken and using two forks pull it apart into strips. Then add to the marinade and thoroughly coat.

5. Next cut the buns in half and pop the under the grill, base side up, and cook for a couple of minutes until browned.

6. Spread the tomato puree over the uncooked side of the buns and then grate the mozzarella and sprinkle evenly over the 8 bun halves. Put back into the grill and cook for a minute or two before adding the chicken to the top of each and cooking for a further few minutes so that the cheese is melted and bubbling underneath.

7. Remove from the heat and top with the spinach, tomatoes and onion.

8. Serve with either a knife and fork or just pick it up with your hands!

Cajun Cod with Sweet Potato Fries & Roasted Vegetables

What better way to make plain fish more interesting but to spice it up! The fish cooks in minutes and the sweet potatoes and vegetables can all just be chopped and thrown in the oven while you do other things.

Easy, quick and a hit with all the family.

I have deliberately not listed quantities for the vegetables as you can eat as many as you like to ensure that you are full.

Ingredients:

SERVES 1

1 piece fresh cod

Sweet potato – 1 small one or ½ large

2 tsp coconut oil

1 clove garlic and/ or 1 fresh red chilli

For the vegetables:

Suggested vegetables: Red onion, Courgette, Peppers, Butternut squash, Aubergine, Mushrooms, Garlic/ chillis, Broccoli

For the cod seasoning:

1 tbsp. Cajun spices/ Cajun style rub

Lime juice – ¼ lime

1 clove minced garlic

1 tsp Oregano

Method

1. Preheat oven to 200 degrees / 180 degrees fan/ gas mark 6.

2. Chop the sweet potato into small wedges or chip size pieces, which ever you prefer. You can keep the skin on especially if you have bought organic – just wash them first and chop off the knobbly edges. Put on a baking tray and drizzle with 1 tbsp. olive oil and place in the oven for about 30-40 minutes until cooked through and golden.

3. Meanwhile chop all vegetables into bite size pieces and place on a baking tray. Drizzle with the rest of the olive oil and sprinkle with 1 clove chopped garlic and/or 1 fresh chilli, chopped. Cook alongside the potatoes in the oven for 20-30 minutes until cooked through. Turn potatoes and veg once whilst cooking to ensure evenly cooked.

4. While the potato and vegetables are cooking prepare the seasoning by combining the ingredients together in small bowl. Rub the ingredients all over the top of the fish with your fingers or a spoon.

5. Heat the coconut oil in a frying pan and once very hot put the fish, seasoned side down, and cook for approx 3 minutes on high heat until seasoning becomes slightly blackened. Then turn the fish over and cook the other side for a few more minutes using any remaining seasoning to flavour it.

6. Serve the fish immediately together with the potatoes and vegetables.

Chicken and Spinach Masala

This is my favourite Friday night meal. A delicious and healthy alternative to a takeaway curry I now actually prefer it!

Also great to serve as an easy dinner party meal with naan, poppadums and rice.

Ingredients:

SERVES 5

1 tsp coconut oil for cooking

1 large or 2 small onions, chopped

3 cloves garlic, chopped

1 chilli, chopped

4 chicken breasts, chopped into bite sized pieces

2 tsps tikka paste (or substitute for your favourite paste)

400g tin tomatoes

cayenne pepper to taste

300g spinach

300g crème fraiche

150g mushrooms (optional but a great way to get an extra portion of veg into your dinner)

Serve with brown basmati or wild rice

Method

1. Heat the coconut oil in a heavy based frying pan and cook the chopped onion, garlic and chilli on low heat until soft but not browned– about 5 minutes.

2. Then add the chicken (and mushrooms if using) to the pan and cook on a higher heat until the outside is browned.

3. Next add the tinned tomatoes, tikka paste and a little cayenne pepper if you like it hot. There is plenty of opportunity to taste later and add more heat if required.

4. Stir through thoroughly before adding the spinach and crème fraiche.

5. Leave to simmer gently, covered, stirring occasionally for 15 minutes or as long as you like until ready to serve.

6. Before serving check spice levels and add more cayenne pepper if required. Tastes delicious with brown rice and a little plain yoghurt swirled in.

Tomatoey Turkey Meatballs with Courgetti

This tasty meatball recipe is just so easy to make and can be cooked early then left bubbling away on the stove until you are ready to eat.

Serve it with courgetti as a low-carb high veg meal option or with brown rice if you need something more filling.

Ingredients:

SERVES 4

2 onions (whichever colour you have is fine)

150g mushrooms

2 tbsp. coconut oil

1 pack of turkey meatballs (contains 12)

2 x 400g tins chopped tomatoes

1/2 rounded tsp paprika

1/2 rounded tsp cayenne pepper (this makes the dish quite spicy so reduce if you don't like so much heat)

2-3 cloves garlic

2 packs courgetti

Method

1. Finely chop the onions and slice the mushrooms ready. Put aside.

2. Heat 1/2 tbsp. coconut oil in a deep sided frying pan and add the meatballs. Cook on a medium to high heat for about 5 minutes until they are browned on the outside. Keep shaking them in the pan to get them browned all over.

3. Once browned remove the meatballs from the pan with a slotted spoon and put aside temporarily.

4. Add another 1/2 tbsp. coconut oil to the pan and gently fry the onions for a few minutes until soft and translucent. Then add the mushrooms and continue to cook for a further few minutes until they take on a shiny sheen.

5. Next add the tinned tomatoes, paprika and cayenne pepper and mix thoroughly. Season to taste.

6. Gently add the meatballs into the tomato mixture, cover them in sauce and reduce the heat leaving them to cook, covered, on a low heat for a minimum of 15 minutes. These can be left for as long as you like to cook as long as they are on a low heat and are stirred occasionally to prevent sticking.

7. Lastly heat the remaining coconut oil in a separate frying pan on a high heat. Add the chopped garlic then the courgetti. Fry on hot, stirring all the time for a few minutes until cooked through. Tip away any water that pools in the pan.

8. Serve the courgetti covered in meatballs and if you are a cheese fan a little parmesan on the top tastes divine!

Drink More Water!

We all know that we should be drinking water but most people just aren't getting enough throughout the day. Plus for every caffeinated or alcoholic drink we consume, and when we exercise, we should be drinking even more.

If you can manage at least two litres a day you will really reap the benefits of improved digestion, clearer skin and more energy. In addition, we often reach for food when in fact we are just thirsty so next time you think you are hungry between meals, try a glass of water instead.

Desserts
& Sweet Treats

Sugar-Free Apple Crumble

I recently asked my followers what traditional foods would they like to see a healthier version of and I was asked to make an apple crumble.

Here's a sugar free version that is super quick to prepare. It's made using rolled oats and desiccated coconut for the topping. It contains a very small amount of high quality maple syrup – feel free to reduce this if you don't want any sweetness at all.

Serve with plain Greek or natural yoghurt.

Ingredients:

SERVES 5

For the filling:

3 Bramley cooking apples (approx. 700g)

75g sultanas (optional -you could always put in blackberries instead)

1/2 tsp cinnamon

6 tbsp. apple juice

1 tsp vanilla bean paste or vanilla extract

For the topping:

150g rolled oats

50g desiccated coconut

1 tsp vanilla bean paste/ vanilla extract

2 tbsp. maple syrup

4 tbsp. coconut oil

Method

1. Preheat oven to 200 degrees / 180 degrees fan/ gas mark 6.

To make the filling:

2. Peel and core the apples and slice to about 1cm thick. Place evenly in the bottom of an ovenproof dish.

3. Add the sultanas (optional) and then sprinkle over the cinnamon, apple juice and vanilla. Mix gently with a fork.

To make the topping:

4. Mix together all the ingredients in a large bowl until evenly mixed.

5. Push down the apples with the fork until packed fairly tightly then pour over the crumble mixture.

6. Cook for 40 minutes in the oven until golden brown on the top.

Sugar-Free Key Lime Pie

This is one of my favourite summer desserts but is always laden with so much sugar I tend to avoid it.

There is no sugar in the recipe, just a little stevia, and instead of using biscuits for the base I have used pecans and desiccated coconut – it's delicious!

Although it's a bit fiddlier than my usual recipes I did manage to make this with a 2 year old 'helping' me!

Ingredients:

SERVES 12

For the base:
1 1/2 cups desiccated coconut (unsweetened if possible)
1 cup pecans
1/4 cup coconut oil, melted
2 mejool dates, destoned
2 tbsp. date syrup

For the topping:
3 limes
1 sachet of gelatine (approx. 12g)
1 1/2 ripe avocados (ensure they are properly ripe or they won't soften and will leave lumps)
200g cream cheese
1/4 cup plain yoghurt
1 cup double cream
2 1/2 tbsp. stevia powder
1 tsp vanilla extract

Method

Base:

1. Put all the base ingredients together in a food processor and mix until combined.

2. Press mixture into a cake tin (approx. 20 cm wide) and put in freezer whilst making the topping.

Topping:

3. Squeeze the juice out of 2 of the limes and put into a small saucepan (but keep hold of the limes as you will need the zest later).

4. Add the gelatine and heat on a low heat until the gelatine has dissolved. Do not allow it to boil. Keep it on very low heat whilst making rest of topping so that it doesn't start to set. Remove from heat only 2 minutes before ready to use it.

5. In a large mixing bowl mix the avocados, cream cheese, yoghurt and double cream together with an electric whisk. Add the stevia, vanilla extract and zest of the 2 limes. Keep whisking until there are no lumps from the avocados and the mixture is completely smooth.

6. Once smooth then pour in the gelatine mixture plus the juice from the 3rd lime.

7. Pour mixture onto the base and top with the zest from the 3rd lime.

8. Leave in the fridge uncovered for 2-3 hours until it has set.

Fruity Yoghurty Dollops!

In the absence of a more descriptive name these became known as dollops!

These are just sooo easy to make and are great fun to do with young kids as they can choose their own healthy toppings and get creative in arranging them how they like.... see what toppings you can come up with.... I've tried grated apple & raisin, pecan nut and goji berry, frozen berries and dried mixed fruit.

Ingredients:

SERVES 2

100g natural or Greek yoghurt (ideally choose high protein and sugar free)

1 tsp stevia (could also use maple syrup or honey if you wish but stevia is the healthier choice)

Toppings:

Choose about 40-50g of the following or make your own combination:

dried mixed fruit

frozen berries

25g raisins / 15g grated apple

25g chopped pecans / 15g goji berries

Extra toppings can be used to decorate the top.

Method

1. Put yoghurt into a bowl and add stevia. Mix.

2. Then add toppings of your choice and combine thoroughly.

3. Turn the mixture out onto a baking tray and flatten.

4. Use some extra toppings to decorate and so you know what's in them.

5. Put into the freezer for 2 hours.

6. When ready to eat remove from freezer and leave for about 2 minutes. Do not leave too long or it will melt!

Sugar-Free Nutty Fudge Bites

These are really easy but very tasty little bites of nuttiness that will curb any sweet cravings and still feel like you've had a treat.

Keep them in the freezer so they are handy whenever you want them.

Ingredients:

MAKES 16

30g butter
30g coconut oil
20g cacao nibs (or just use very dark chocolate)
150g pecan nuts
4 medjool dates, destoned
cocoa powder for dusting

Method

1. Line a small, square tray or dish (it doesn't matter too much what you use but square just helps with cutting).

2. Melt the butter, coconut oil and cacao nibs (or chocolate) in a bowl in the microwave for 1 minute.

3. The add the melted mixture along with the nuts and dates into a food processor and blend for a few minutes until the texture of coarse sand.

4. Scrape into the lined dish and flatten down.

5. Pop into the freezer for an hour and then take out and cut into squares (if you prefer you could always make into balls before freezing).

6. Dust each square in cocoa powder and then either serve or pop back in the dish and keep in the freezer until required.

Sugar-Free Fruity Carrot Cake

I was given this recipe on a recent course, adapted from a Nigella recipe.

The sugar, butter and flour have all been replaced by healthier alternatives so although it remains a treat, you can indulge without the guilt!

If you haven't come across stevia before it is a plant based sweetener that doesn't effect your blood sugar levels like other sugars.

Prep time approx. 20 mins, cooking time 30-40 minutes

Ingredients:

MAKES 20 SQUARES

3 tbsp. pine nuts

2 medium carrots, approx. 250g

75g sultanas

60ml dark rum, brandy or orange juice

150g stevia but you can also use xylitol if preferred

125g olive oil (and yes grams is correct)

1 tsp vanilla extract

3 large eggs

250g ground almonds

1/2 tsp nutmeg

juice and finely grated zest of 1/2 lemon

Method

1. Preheat oven to 180 degrees / 160 degrees fan/ gas mark 4.

2. Grease and line a square tin approx. 23cm wide.

3. Put the pine nuts into a small frying pan and toast over a medium to high heat until golden brown. Ensure you keep them moving the whole time or they will burn very quickly.

4. If possible grate the carrots using the fine grating disc on a food processor. If not grate by hand. Then spread on double thickness kitchen roll or a clean tea towel to absorb as much moisture as possible.

5. Meanwhile put the sultanas and rum into a small saucepan and simmer gently until most of the liquid has been absorbed (less than 5 minutes).

6. Whisk the stevia, olive oil and eggs (ideally with an electric whisk as it will be much quicker and easier!) until creamy, light and airy.

7. Then whisk in the vanilla and fold in the ground almonds, nutmeg, carrots and sultanas with any remaining rum from the pan. Finally stir in the lemon zest and juice. Mix thoroughly but gently.

8. Turn the cake mixture out into the tin and level the surface with a spatula. Scatter the pine nuts over the top and put into the oven for 30 to 40 minutes. The cake is cooked when the top is risen and golden and a skewer comes out sticky but more or less clean.

9. Remove from the oven and let the cake sit on a wire rack for 10 minutes before removing from the tin. Leave on the rack to cool completely before cutting.

Cranberry and Nut Snack Bars

These are a great snack option full of filling nuts and seeds and containing plenty of protein and good fats to keep you full.

If you are watching your sugar intake ensure you get unsweetened cranberries and reduce the amount of honey – they still taste delicious.

You can also change around the nuts and seeds depending on whatever you have in your cupboard, mine tend to differ every time I make them!

Ingredients:

MAKES 18 SLICES OR
16 MINI SQUARES

coconut or olive oil for greasing

35g desiccated coconut

45g pecans, chopped or just break with your hands

30g pistachios

30g pumpkin seeds

20g chopped hazelnuts

20g flaxseed mix (Linwoods do a good one available from most supermarkets in the baking aisle)

15g sunflower seeds

5g chia seeds

50g unsweetened cranberries

pinch sea salt or Himalayan salt

40g coconut oil, melted

50 g honey

Method

1. Preheat oven to 200 degrees / 180 degrees fan/ gas mark 6.

2. Line an oven dish with greaseproof paper and lightly grease on top with coconut oil or olive oil (the dish I used was 24cm square).

3. Put the coconut, pecans, pistachios, pumpkin seeds, hazelnuts, flaxseed and chia seeds into a dry frying pan on high heat and cook for a few minutes stirring constantly to ensure it doesn't burn. Remove from heat once starting to brown.

4. Tip the nut mixture into a large mixing bowl and add the cranberries and salt. Then add the honey and coconut oil and stir until evenly mixed.

5. Transfer the mixture into your dish and press down firmly or it will fall apart later!

6. Bake for 20 minutes in the oven until golden brown on top. Then remove from oven and leave in the dish to cool but press it down firmly once more.

7. Leave to cool in dish for about an hour before slicing.

About Me

Who Was I?

An ambitious, outgoing and successful woman with a wonderful husband, hectic social life and a thriving career. But deep down I wasn't happy or fulfilled with my life and I couldn't work out why.

Only now do I realise that I was so exhausted trying to keep everything running perfectly, and every ball in the air at once, that I was forgetting to look after myself and wasn't the healthy happy person I deserved to be.

I got through it by using food! Sugar became my comfort and I relied on it to help me deal with stress and to keep me awake as I was so exhausted.

I hit an all time low after being made redundant as not only had I lost the job I was good at, it took away my identity and my self-esteem.

It was only when I read about the impact of the maternal diet on children did it shock me into realising that I needed to change not only for myself but for my family too.

What Changed?

Being made redundant gave me the opportunity to pursue my dream of giving something back and helping people with their health and wellness.

Initially I just started studying as something to keep my brain busy whilst the rest of my time was taken dealing with a tiny baby. I started studying nutrition with no idea of where it was taking me at first but the more I learnt the more I wanted to learn. After much deliberation I decided to study Health Coaching so that I could utilise my people skills with my health training and be able to give something back to women like me so that they can change their lives and become healthier happier versions of themselves.

At the same time I took myself and my husband on the start of our own health journey. We became my first clients and transformed our lives. We have changed our mind-sets, habits and behaviour around food and now lead a healthier lifestyle waking up in the morning excited and raring to go.

I finally feel good about myself and I am excited to share this wonderful health secret with you all.

TURN YOUR BOOK DREAMS

INTO A REALITY

Do you have an idea for a book you've always wanted to create.

Are your friends and family always saying, "you should be an author?"

Old Mate Media specialises in helping indie authors self-publish their ideas and own 100% of the copyright. We will walk you down the path to being published.

VISIT WWW.OLDMATEMEDIA.COM FOR DETAILS

Tell Us What You Think

If you enjoyed the recipes in Eat Well, Feel Great; we would love you to pop online and leave a review on Amazon or Facebook. Reviews will help others people find and enjoy these delicious meals.

For Amazon:
Search "Eat Well, Feel Great" in the search bar
Click on the book page
Scroll down to where it says Customer Reviews
Click on Write a Customer Review
Note: You'll need to be logged in to your Amazon account

For Facebook
Search "Vitality Health Coaching" in the search bar
Click on Reviews on the left hand side
Give a star rating, add your review and click Done

Printed in Poland
by Amazon Fulfillment
Poland Sp. z o.o., Wrocław